the

orient
express
book

charmaine solomon

HAMLYN

First published in Great Britain
in 1998 by Hamlyn
an imprint of Reed International
Books Limited
Michelin House, 81 Fulham Road
London SW3 6RB
and Auckland, Melbourne,
Singapore and Toronto

Published 1997 by Hamlyn Australia
a part of Reed Books Australia
35 Cotham Rd, Kew
Victoria 3101
a division of Reed International
Books Australia Pty Limited

First published in 1993 by Hamlyn
Australia as part of Charmaine Solomon's
Asian Cooking Library

ISBN for UK edition 0 600 59467 X

A CIP catalogue for this book is available
from the British Library

National Library of Australia
cataloguing-in-publication data:

Solomon, Charmaine.
   The orient express book.
   Includes index.
   ISBN for Australian edition
   0 947334 73 4
   1. Quick and easy cookery.
   2. Cookery, Asian.
   I. Title.

641.555

Designed by Guy Mirabella
Photographs by Michael Cook, Reg
Morrison and Rodney Weidland
Styling by Margaret Alcock
Food cooked by Nina Harris, Jill Pavey
China: Villeroy & Boch, Australia
Pty Ltd

Quark XPress by Melbourne
Media Services
Printed and bound in China by
Mandarin Book Production

A Metric/Imperial guide to Australian solid and liquid measures

Liquid Measures

Australian	Metric	Imperial
1 cup	250 ml	8 fl oz
1/2 cup	125 ml	4 fl oz
1/3 cup	75 ml	3 fl oz

Solid Measures

Australian	Metric	Imperial
1 cup	300 g	10 oz
1/2 cup	150 g	5 oz
1/3 cup	125 g	4 oz

Liquid Measures/Teaspoons/Tablespoons

A teaspoon holds approximately 5 ml in both
Australia and Britain. The British standard tablespoon
holds 15 ml, whilst the Australian holds 20 ml.

Australian	British
1 teaspoon	1 teaspoon
1 tablespoon	1 tablespoon
2 tablespoons	2 tablespoons
3 1/2 tablespoons	3 tablespoons
4 tablespoons	3 1/2 tablespoons

Notes

Convert cup measures to metric or
imperial measures where necessary.
Use one set of measurements only and
not a mixture. Standard level spoon
measurements are used in all recipes.
Eggs should be medium (size 3) unless
otherwise stated.
Milk should be full fat unless otherwise stated.
Pepper should be freshly milled unless
otherwise stated.
Fresh herbs should be used unless otherwise
stated. If unavailable use dried herbs as an
alternative but halve the quantities stated.

For ease of reference:
Capsicum = Pepper
Eggplant = Aubergine
Zucchini = Courgette

contents

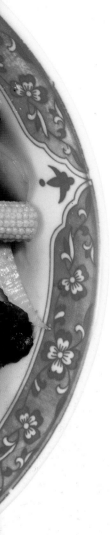

soups

chicken

and sweetcorn soup

serves 6

Preparation: 20 mins
Cooking: 10 mins

250 g (8 oz) chicken tenderloin or
    breast fillet
½ teaspoon salt
2 egg whites, beaten to a froth
3 tablespoons cornflour
1.5 litres (3 pints) Chicken Stock
    (see Basics p. 90)
1 tablespoon light soy sauce
2 tablespoons dry sherry
1 × 440 g (15 oz) can creamed
    corn
1 teaspoon oriental sesame oil
1 spring onion, finely sliced
½ cup shredded ham

Trim the white sinew from the chicken tenderloins and
mince or chop so finely that the flesh is almost a purée.
Add salt, 2 teaspoons cornflour and a tablespoon of cold
water and mix well. Fold in the egg whites.

Bring the Chicken Stock to the boil. Add the remaining
cornflour blended with 60 ml (2 fl oz) cold water, stirring until
stock returns to the boil. Boil for 1 to 2 minutes until it thickens.
Add the soy sauce, sherry and corn and stir. Add the sesame oil and
puréed chicken and stir gently as it simmers for 1 to 2 minutes. Serve
garnished with spring onion and ham.

lentil and vegetable soup

A fairly thick soup with a pronounced sour and spicy flavour.

serves 6

Preparation: 10 mins
Cooking: 30 mins

220 g (7 oz) red lentils
1 tablespoon tamarind pulp or
   1 teaspoon instant tamarind
   (see Note)
1 tablespoon oil
1 tablespoon ground coriander
2 teaspoons ground cummin
¼ teaspoon ground black pepper
½ teaspoon ground turmeric
⅛ teaspoon asafoetida, optional

3 cups mixed vegetables
   (zucchini, eggplants, beans,
   pumpkin—cut into bite-sized
   pieces)
2 fresh green chillies, seeded and
   sliced
½ teaspoon black mustard seeds
1 small onion, finely sliced
   salt to taste

Wash the lentils well and drain. Simmer in 1.5 litres (3 pints) water until soft. Soak tamarind pulp in 250 ml (8 fl oz) hot water for 5 minutes and squeeze to dissolve pulp. Strain, discarding seeds and fibres (or dissolve instant tamarind in hot water). Add liquid to the lentils.

In another heavy saucepan heat 2 teaspoons of oil and fry ground spices and asafoetida over a very low heat, stirring, for 1 to 2 minutes. Pour the lentil mixture into this pan; add the vegetables and chillies and simmer until vegetables are cooked.

Heat the remaining oil in a small, heavy frying pan and fry the mustard seeds and onion until the seeds pop and the onion is brown. Stir frequently so that the onion does not burn. Stir into the soup, salt to taste, simmer a few minutes longer and serve as a first course or with steamed rice.

Note If tamarind is difficult to obtain, lime or lemon juice can be substituted. Use enough to give a distinctly tart flavour.

miso soup

Miso is a Japanese fermented soy bean paste that comes in different varieties according to the type of malt added. For the slimmer it is ideal, being low in kilojoules but satisfying and flavoursome at the same time. The miso is combined with dashi (a bonito fish stock) and tofu and/or different vegetable garnishes.

serves 6

Preparation: 5 mins
Cooking: 5 mins

1 small leek
12 button mushrooms
1.5 litres (3 pints) liquid dashi (or use instant dashi and follow instructions on the label)
3 tablespoons miso

Wash the leek well and slice into thin rounds. Wipe the mushroom caps, trim the stems and cut into thin slices. Bring dashi to the boil in a saucepan. Put miso into a ladle and immerse the ladle slowly into the broth, stirring constantly with chopsticks until the miso dissolves (or dissolve in a small bowl using a spoon if you prefer). Mix the dissolved miso gradually into the broth, making sure there are no lumps. Add the leek and mushrooms. As soon as the broth boils again, remove from the heat—it is important not to overcook the miso since overcooking destroys its aroma.

egg flower soup

This Chinese soup takes its name from the fact that the beaten egg looks like chrysanthemum petals when poured into boiling stock.

serves 4

Preparation: 5 mins
Cooking: 5 mins

1 litre (2 pints) Chicken Stock (see Basics p. 90)
2 tablespoons dry sherry
1 teaspoon oriental sesame oil salt to taste

2 eggs, beaten
2 spring onions, finely sliced

Bring stock to the boil. Add the sherry, sesame oil, and salt if necessary. Slowly pour the beaten egg into the boiling stock. Stir once or twice. Serve immediately, sprinkled with spring onions.

chicken and bean curd soup

serves 6

Preparation: 20 mins
Soaking: 30 mins
    (if using dried shiitake
    mushrooms)
Cooking: 5 mins

6 dried or fresh shiitake (Chinese)
    mushrooms
6 teaspoons soy sauce
1½ teaspoons sugar
3 chicken breast fillets
3 squares fresh bean curd
1.5 litres (3 pints) Chicken Stock
    (see Basics p. 90)
3 spring onions, finely sliced
    few drops oriental sesame oil

Soak the dried mushrooms in hot water for 30 minutes. Cut off and discard the stems.

Reserve the soaking water. Cut the caps in thin slices; put in a small pan with 180 ml (6 fl oz) of water (or reserved liquid), the soy sauce and sugar. Bring to the boil and cook until almost all the liquid has evaporated.

Cut the chicken fillets into small dice. Slice each bean curd square into 3 strips, then across

to make equal-sized dice. Bring the Chicken Stock to the boil, add the chicken and simmer for 1 minute. Add the mushrooms and bean curd and bring back to a simmer. Add the spring onions and sesame oil. Remove from the heat and cover. Leave to stand for 1 minute, then serve.

beef soup with salad

An unusual combination, this Vietnamese recipe makes a complete meal in a bowl—its success depends on a really strong stock.

serves 6

Preparation: 20 mins
Freezing: 60 mins
  (optional)
Cooking: 10 mins

2 litres (4 pints) Beef Stock
  (see Basics p. 90)
  salt to taste
375 g (12 oz) packet dried rice
  noodles or 1 kg (2 lb) fresh
  rice noodles (Banh Pho)
250 g (8 oz) fresh bean sprouts
4 spring onions

3 firm ripe tomatoes
2 white onions
500 g (1 lb) rump or fillet steak
  fish sauce
  lemon wedges
  fresh red chillies, chopped
  fresh coriander leaves, chopped
  fresh mint leaves

Soak the rice noodles in hot water for 10 minutes or boil for 2 minutes. Drain.

Rinse the bean sprouts with cold water and pinch off any straggly roots. Slice the spring onions finely.

Cut the tomatoes in half lengthwise, then slice each half. Peel and thinly slice the white onions. Slice steak into paper-thin, bite-sized pieces (this is easier if you partially freeze the meat until just firm).

Put a serving of noodles and a handful of bean sprouts in each large soup bowl. Place a few

slices of beef, tomato and onions in a large ladle; immerse the ladle in boiling stock until the beef is pink—do not overcook. Pour contents of ladle over noodles and bean sprouts. Add fish sauce, a squeeze of lemon juice, chillies, coriander and mint leaves to individual bowls to taste.

thai
pumpkin and coconut soup

Make sure the pumpkin you select is ripe—brightly coloured, with a firm texture and sweet flavour. Buy cut pumpkin if you're unsure, because what you see is what you get.

serves 6

Preparation: 10 mins
Soaking: 10 mins
Cooking: 25 mins

750 g (1½ lb) ripe pumpkin
½ cup dried shrimp
3 shallots or 1 small onion, chopped
2 stems lemon grass, tender white
    part only, finely chopped (or
    zest of 1 lemon, finely peeled)
250 ml (8 fl oz) canned coconut milk
1 tablespoon fish sauce
lime juice to taste
250 ml (8 fl oz) Chicken Stock,
    optional (see Basics p. 90)
few fresh basil leaves

Peel and dice the pumpkin. Soak the dried shrimp in hot water for 10 minutes. Place the drained shrimp with the shallots and lemon grass in a blender or food processor and purée with a little water. Combine purée with 125 ml (4 fl oz) coconut milk and 375 ml (12 fl oz) water and bring to the boil, stirring constantly. Simmer for 5 minutes. Add the pumpkin and simmer until tender. Stir in the remaining coconut milk and bring back to the boil. Add the fish sauce and lime juice to taste. (If you prefer thinner soup add a little hot Chicken Stock.) Throw in basil leaves just before taking off the heat.

chicken
dumpling soup

serves 6

Preparation: 20 mins
Cooking: 10 mins

250 g (8 oz) minced chicken
2 spring onions, finely sliced
½ teaspoon salt
1 tablespoon soy sauce
1 clove garlic, crushed
¼ teaspoon finely grated fresh
   ginger
125 g (4 oz) wonton wrappers
2 litres (4 pints) Chicken Stock
   (see Basics p. 90)
chopped fresh coriander to
   garnish

Mix together the chicken, spring onions, salt, soy sauce, garlic and ginger. Place
small teaspoons of this filling on each wonton wrapper. Moisten the edges of the
wrapper and fold diagonally over filling to make a triangle, pressing the edges
together to seal. Moisten two corners at the base of the triangle and then press them
together.

Bring stock to the boil in a large pan and add dumplings. Stir until boiling again,
then simmer for 10 minutes. Serve immediately garnished with coriander.

soup with meatballs

serves 4

Preparation: 10 mins
Cooking: 12 mins

375 g (12 oz) minced pork
½ teaspoon finely grated fresh
   ginger
1 clove garlic, crushed
   salt to taste
2 tablespoons finely chopped
   spring onions

2 slices soft white bread, crumbed
1 egg yolk
1.5 litres (3 pints) Chicken Stock
   (see Basics p. 90)
1 tablespoon dry sherry
3 teaspoons cornflour
1 teaspoon oriental sesame oil
2 spring onions, thinly sliced

Mix the pork with the ginger, garlic, salt, spring onions, breadcrumbs and egg yolk. Form teaspoons of the mixture into balls. Bring the stock to the boil, drop in the balls, cover and simmer for 10 minutes, then remove with a slotted spoon.

Mix the sherry with the cornflour and 2 tablespoons of cold water and add to the simmering stock. Boil, stirring, for about 1 minute, or until the soup is clear and slightly thickened. Stir in the sesame oil. Return the meatballs to the soup and serve garnished with spring onions.

lamb & beef

stir-fried lamb with vegetables

serves 4

Preparation: 15 mins
Soaking: 30 mins
   (If using dried shiitake
   mushrooms)
Marinating: 30 mins
Cooking: 8 mins

6 fresh or dried shiitake (Chinese)
   mushrooms
500 g (1 lb) lamb leg steaks or lamb
   fillets
½ teaspoon crushed garlic
   salt to taste
2 teaspoons grated fresh ginger
1 teaspoon oriental sesame oil
1 tablespoon dry sherry

1 egg white, slightly beaten
   cornflour
2 tablespoons peanut oil
2 sticks celery, sliced
1 cup snow peas or sugar snap
   peas, strings removed
1 white onion, cut in wedges
2 tablespoons soy sauce
1 teaspoon sugar

Soak the dried mushrooms in hot water for 30 minutes. Discard stalks and slice caps. Trim any fat from the lamb, slice the meat thinly and place in a bowl. Combine garlic, salt, ginger, sesame oil, sherry, egg white and 1 tablespoon cornflour. Mix with the lamb, cover and leave to marinate for 30 minutes.

Heat 1 tablespoon peanut oil and fry celery and mushroom slices for 1 minute, add snow peas and onion, fry a minute longer. Remove to a plate. Add the remaining oil to the wok and when hot add lamb, tossing and stirring constantly. Mix together soy sauce, sugar and 1 teaspoon cornflour with 60 ml (2 fl oz) water. Push the meat aside, add the sauce mixture and cook, stirring, until thickened. Return the vegetables to the wok and mix with the lamb and sauce. Serve hot with rice or noodles.

shredded beef with asparagus

Lamb fillets would make a tasty variation to this dish.

serves 4

Preparation: 10 mins
Marinating: 20 mins
Cooking: 3 mins

500 g (1 lb) grilling steak
2 onions
1 bunch asparagus
4 tablespoons peanut oil

Marinade

2 teaspoons dark soy sauce
2 teaspoons cornflour
1 teaspoon sugar
4 teaspoons dry sherry

Sauce

4 teaspoons light soy sauce
4 teaspoons oyster sauce
2 teaspoons cornflour

Cut the onions in half lengthwise, then cut each half lengthwise into four wedges. Snap any tough ends off the asparagus and discard. Cut stalks diagonally into 5-cm (2-in) lengths.

Combine Marinade ingredients and mix well into meat. Leave to marinate for about 20 minutes. Mix Sauce ingredients with 2 tablespoons water. Heat wok, add 2 teaspoons of peanut oil and stir-fry onions over high heat for 1 minute. With a slotted spoon transfer onions to a plate. Add the asparagus to the wok and stir-fry, tossing for 1 minute. Remove the asparagus to a plate. Add the remaining tablespoons of oil to the wok and, when hot, add meat and stir-fry, tossing over high heat until it changes colour. Put meat aside with onions.

Wipe out the wok and return asparagus to it. Add 4 tablespoons hot water. Cover wok and cook for 3 minutes or until asparagus is tender but still crisp. Add Sauce mixture and stir until it boils and thickens slightly. Return beef and onions to the wok and toss together until heated through. Serve at once with rice.

quick-cooked beef and vegetables

A low-fat adaptation of the Japanese sukiyaki. If you have an electric frying pan, you can cook the dish at the table. Guests then help themselves from the pan. You will need a very tender steak for this dish—aged rump steak would be a good substitute for fillet.

serves 6

Preparation: 30 mins
Freezing: 60 mins
 (optional)
Cooking: 10 mins

1 kg (2 lb) fillet steak or tender
 rump, in one piece
3 small leeks
1 × 565 g (1¼ lb) can baby corn
 cobs
250 g (8 oz) button mushrooms or
 canned shiitake (Chinese)
 mushrooms
3 white onions

250 g (8 oz) fresh bean sprouts
1 small Chinese white cabbage
60 g (2 oz) bean thread vermicelli
6 squares bean curd (tofu)
 oil for greasing pan
 Japanese soy sauce
 sugar
 sake (Japanese rice wine)
 Beef Stock
 (see Basics p.90)

Cut steak into paper-thin slices (this is easier if you partially freeze the meat until just firm). Cut the leeks into diagonal slices and drain the corn cobs. Wipe the mushroom caps, trim stalks and cut into halves. Peel the onions and cut in small wedges. Wash and drain the bean sprouts and pinch off the tails. Discard the outer leaves and cut the Chinese cabbage into bite-sized pieces. Cook the noodles in boiling water for 10 minutes, drain. Set out all the ingredients on a large platter.

Heat a large heavy frying pan and rub with a little oil. Add half of each vegetable to the pan and fry on high heat until just tender. Push to one side and add slices of meat in one layer. When cooked on one side (this will only take a short time because meat is so thinly sliced) turn and cook other side. Sprinkle with soy sauce, sugar and sake to taste. Add a little stock to moisten the meat and vegetables. Mix in half the noodles and tofu and heat through. Serve immediately in individual bowls with hot steamed rice.

Remaining ingredients are added to the pan and cooked after the first batch has been eaten.

five
-spice beef with vegetables

Keep the vegetables crisp and crunchy and watch them disappear.

serves 4

Preparation: 15 mins
Freezing: 60 mins
  (optional)
Cooking: 4 mins

750 g (1½ lb) rump steak
½ teaspoon crushed garlic
1 teaspoon finely grated fresh ginger
½ teaspoon five-spice powder
1 cup broccoli florets
1 large red capsicum
2 teaspoons cornflour
1 tablespoon dark soy sauce
1 tablespoon dry sherry
2 tablespoons peanut oil
1 teaspoon oriental sesame oil
3 spring onions, sliced diagonally

Trim the beef of any fat and cut into paper-thin slices (this is easier if you partially freeze the meat until just firm). Combine the garlic, ginger and five-spice powder with the beef.

Blanch the broccoli in lightly salted boiling water for 1 minute, drain immediately. Slice capsicum in strips, discarding seeds. Combine cornflour, soy and sherry with 60 ml (2 fl oz) cold water.

Heat the peanut oil in the wok and stir-fry the capsicum for 30 seconds. Push aside and stir-fry meat, tossing until it changes colour. Stir sauce and cornflour mixture again and add to wok, stirring until it boils and thickens. Add broccoli, toss to combine all the vegetables and meat with the sauce and finally add sesame oil and spring onions and stir through. Serve at once with rice.

vietnamese

stir-fried beef with sesame sauce

serves 4

Preparation: 10 mins
Freezing: 60 mins
  (optional)
Cooking: 5 mins

375 g (12 oz) lean grilling steak
2 tablespoons soy sauce
60 ml (2 fl oz) peanut oil
1 teaspoon crushed garlic
125 ml (4 fl oz) Beef Stock
  (see Basics p. 90)
3 teaspoons cornflour
2 teaspoons hot chilli sauce
3 teaspoons toasted sesame paste
  (see Note) or smooth peanut
  butter
2 teaspoons toasted sesame
  seeds

With a sharp knife, shred the beef as thinly as possible (this is easier if you partially freeze the meat until just firm). In a wok, heat the oil and stir-fry the meat with the garlic on a high heat for 2 to 3 minutes until the meat changes colour. Add the stock and when boiling, add the cornflour blended to a smooth paste with a little cold water. Stir until it boils and thickens. Turn off the heat and stir in the chilli sauce and sesame paste. Sprinkle with sesame seeds and serve with boiled rice.

Note Sesame paste is the Chinese variety, not Middle Eastern tahini, which is made from raw sesame seeds.

spinach and lamb curry

Serve this aromatic curry with rice, or Indian bread and fresh chutney.

serves 4

Preparation: 15 mins
Cooking: 40 mins

500 g (1 lb) lamb fillets
1 large bunch spinach, well washed or 1 packet frozen spinach
1 large onion, roughly chopped
1 tablespoon chopped fresh ginger
2 large cloves garlic, chopped

4 dried red chillies
3 tablespoons oil or ghee
½ teaspoon kalonji (nigella seeds)
salt to taste
5 cardamom pods, bruised
125 ml (4 fl oz) plain yoghurt
¼ teaspoon ground black pepper

Trim off any fat and cut the meat into cubes. Chop the spinach roughly. Purée the onion, ginger, galic and chillies (broken into pieces) in a blender, adding a little water if necessary.

Heat the oil or ghee in a heavy saucepan and fry the kalonji seeds for 1 minute. Add the blended mixture and fry, stirring, until it browns and oil starts to separate from mixture—about 10 minutes. Stir in the meat until cubes are well coated. Cover and cook on a low heat until juices come out of the meat. Add the spinach, salt and cardamom pods. Cover and cook until liquid is absorbed and meat is tender. Remove from the heat, stir in yoghurt and pepper.

stir-fried chilli beef with asparagus

serves 4 to 6

Preparation: 20 mins
Freezing: 60 mins
 (optional)
Cooking: 4 mins

500 g (1 lb) lean steak, rump or fillet
1 clove garlic crushed with
 ½ teaspoon salt
1 teaspoon finely grated fresh
 ginger
2 tablespoons peanut oil
1 red capsicum, seeded
250 g (8 oz) tender green asparagus
1 white onion, peeled and cut in
 6 wedges
2 teaspoons cornflour
2 tablespoons light soy sauce
1 teaspoon hot chilli sauce
1 teaspoon oriental sesame oil

Cut beef into paper-thin slices (this is easier if you partially freeze the meat until just firm). Rub the crushed garlic and ginger into the beef. Cut the capsicum into strips. Slice the asparagus diagonally into bite-sized pieces. Cut the onion wedges in halves crossways and separate the layers. Combine cornflour, soy sauce, chilli sauce, sesame oil and 85 ml (2½ fl oz) water.

Heat the wok, add 1 tablespoon of oil and fry the vegetables on a high heat for 1 minute. Remove from the wok. Add the remaining oil and stir-fry the meat for 2 minutes or until no longer pink. Stir the cornflour mixture and add, stirring constantly until it boils and thickens. Return the vegetables and stir through. Serve immediately with rice.

garlic beef and mustard cabbage

Lamb fillets would make a tasty variation to this dish.

serves 4

Preparation: 20 mins
Soaking: 30 mins
  (if using dried shiitake
  mushrooms)
Cooking: 5 mins

500 g (1 lb) fillet or rump steak
8 dried or fresh shiitake (Chinese)
  mushrooms
250 g (8 oz) mustard cabbage
  (gai choy)
4 tablespoons dark soy sauce
2 tablespoons sugar
4 cloves garlic
  salt to taste
4 tablespoons peanut oil
2 teaspoons oriental sesame oil

Sauce

4 teaspoons dry sherry
4 teaspoons dark soy sauce
2 tablespoons oyster sauce
1 teaspoon sugar
2 teaspoons cornflour

Remove any fat from the steak and slice the meat thinly across the grain. Soak the dried mushrooms in hot water for 30 minutes. Discard the stems, cut caps into halves and simmer for 15 minutes in water (or reserved liquid) with soy sauce and sugar. Drain. Wash the cabbage well and drain. Discard any tough ends of outer leaves and slice the cabbage diagonally. Crush the garlic with a little salt. Combine the Sauce ingredients in a small bowl.

Heat a wok, add 2 tablespoons of the peanut oil and swirl to coat. Add the steak and stir-fry over a high heat, tossing until the colour changes. Remove to a plate. Add the remaining peanut oil to the wok. When hot, add the cabbage, garlic and mushrooms and stir-fry for 1 minute. Return the meat to the wok and continue to cook for 30 seconds. Add the Sauce mixture and stir through. Remove from the heat and stir in sesame oil. Serve immediately with rice.

beef
with peanut sauce

serves 4

Preparation: 10 mins
Cooking: 6 mins

375 g (12 oz) rump steak
3 tablespoons peanut oil
½ teaspoon crushed garlic
2 cups shredded Chinese white
    cabbage
3 spring onions, finely sliced
125 ml (4 fl oz) Beef Stock
    (see Basics p. 90)
1 tablespoon fish sauce
3 teaspoons cornflour
1 tablespoon smooth peanut
    butter

Slice the steak thinly. Heat the peanut oil in a wok, add the meat and garlic and stir-fry over a high heat for 2 minutes. Remove from the wok and set aside. Add the cabbage and spring onions and toss over a high heat for 1 minute. Return the meat, add the stock and fish sauce and bring to the boil. Push the food to the side of the wok. Mix the cornflour with 2 tablespoons cold water until smooth, add to the liquid and stir until it boils and thickens. Stir in the peanut butter. Serve with rice.

steak
in plum sauce

serves 6

Preparation: 10 mins
Marinating: 60 mins
Cooking: 8 mins

500 g (1 lb) fillet or other tender steak
2 tablespoons light soy sauce
1 tablespoon dry sherry
1 teaspoon grated ginger
1 clove garlic, crushed with ½ teaspoon salt
6 spring onions
1 tablespoon oil
2 tablespoons plum sauce
finely shredded lettuce

Remove any fat from the beef. Cut across into 6 slices. Flatten slices with the blade of a cleaver. Mix soy sauce, sherry, ginger and garlic. Place the beef in a bowl and pour the mixture over, turning slices so that they are well coated. Leave to marinate for at least 1 hour.

Slice the spring onions into bite-sized pieces. Heat a wok, add half the oil and swirl to coat the surface. When hot fry 3 slices of beef, pressing against wok to brown both sides. Remove and reserve. Add the remaining oil and cook the remaining beef. Add the spring onions, return first 3 slices of meat and toss briefly. Stir in plum sauce with 2 tablespoons of water and heat through. Serve on a bed of finely shredded lettuce.

stir-fried beef and cucumbers

serves 6

Preparation: 15 mins
Freezing: 60 mins
(optional)
Cooking: 5 mins

375 g (12 oz) lean rump or fillet
   steak
1 teaspoon oriental sesame oil
1½ tablespoons light soy sauce
½ teaspoon sugar
¼ teaspoon cayenne pepper
2 green cucumbers
1 tablespoon oil
1 tablespoon crushed sesame
   seeds, toasted

Trim off any fat and cut steak into paper-thin slices (this is easier if you partially freeze the
meat until just firm). Slices should be about 5 cm (2 in) long and 12 mm (½ in) wide. Put the beef in
a bowl and mix in the sesame oil, soy sauce, sugar and cayenne. Make sure the meat is well coated
so that the flavours penetrate.

Peel the cucumbers, but leave a thin strip of green at intervals to give a decorative effect.
Cut in halves lengthwise and scoop out seeds with a small spoon. Cut across into thin slices.

Heat oil in a wok, swirling to coat the surface. Add the beef and stir-fry on a high heat for
1 minute. Add cucumbers and toss for a further minute. Let the mixture simmer until the cucumber is
half cooked. It should be tender but still crisp. Garnish with sesame seeds and serve immediately.

chilli beef with celery

Lamb fillets would make a tasty variation to this dish.

serves 4

Preparation: 10 mins
Cooking: 5 mins

500 g (1 lb) lean grilling steak
4 stalks celery
4 teaspoons canned salted black
beans
4 teaspoons dark soy sauce
2 teaspoons chilli bean sauce
1 teaspoon sugar
2 teaspoons cornflour
4 tablespoons peanut oil
2 teaspoons crushed garlic

Remove any fat from the meat and slice the steak thinly across the grain. Wash the celery and cut across into 1.5-cm (½-in) slices. Rinse the black beans under cold water, drain and chop. Mix the soy sauce, chilli bean sauce, sugar and cornflour with 4 tablespoons cold water.

Heat a wok and add 2 tablespoons of oil, swirling to coat the inside. Stir-fry beef over a high heat, tossing until browned. Remove to a plate. Add the remaining oil and stir-fry celery for 2 minutes. Remove with slotted spoon. Add the garlic to the oil remaining in the pan and stir-fry for a few seconds. Add the black beans and stir-fry for a few seconds more. Stir in sauce mixture, cooking until it boils and thickens. Return the celery to the wok and simmer for 2 minutes. Add the beef and stir until reheated through. Serve immediately with hot steamed rice.

chicken & pork

thai
chicken with snow peas

serves 4

Preparation: 10 mins
Cooking: 15 mins

500 g (1 lb) chicken thigh fillets
125 g (4 oz) snow peas
125 ml (4 fl oz) canned coconut milk
2 tablespoons Thai Green Curry
   Paste (see Basics p. 90)
1 tablespoon fish sauce
1 teaspoon palm sugar or brown
   sugar
4 kaffir lime leaves
¼ cup sweet basil leaves

Trim excess fat from the chicken and cut into bite-sized pieces. Top and string the snow peas.

Heat half the coconut milk in a wok. When boiling add Thai Green Curry Paste and cook, stirring for a few minutes. Add the fish sauce and chicken pieces and cook, stirring constantly, until the chicken is well coated and no longer pink.

Mix the remaining coconut milk with 125 ml (4 fl oz) water and add to the wok with sugar and kaffir lime leaves. Simmer over a low heat for 10 minutes. Add snow peas and basil and simmer a few minutes more. Serve with hot white rice.

chilli
pork with broccoli

500 g (1 lb) pork fillet or other lean
     pork
375 g (12 oz) broccoli
  1 tablespoon canned, salted black
     beans
  1 tablespoon dark soy sauce
  2 teaspoons chilli bean sauce
  1 teaspoon sugar
  1 teaspoon cornflour
  1 tablespoon peanut oil
  1 clove garlic, crushed
    red chilli, finely sliced

Remove any fat from the pork and cut into paper-thin slices (this is easier if you partially freeze the meat until just firm). Cut the broccoli into bite-sized pieces and blanch in boiling water for 1 minute. Drain and set aside. Rinse the black beans under cold water, drain and chop. Combine the soy sauce, chilli bean sauce, sugar and cornflour with 4 tablespoons cold water.

Heat a wok, add the oil and swirl to coat the surface. Add the pork and stir-fry over a high heat, tossing until browned. Remove the pork and set aside. Add the garlic and chopped black beans; stir-fry for a few seconds. Stir in the sauce mixture and cook until it boils and thickens. Return the pork to the wok with the broccoli and stir together until heated through. Serve immediately, garnished with chilli.

chicken
in black bean sauce

In a stir-fried recipe like this one, the preparation is just as important as the cooking. Having everything measured, ready and within reach is the secret behind this Chinese technique, surely one of the fastest cooking methods known.

serves 4

Preparation: 15 mins
Cooking: 5 mins

500 g (1 lb) chicken breast fillet
3 stalks celery
2 teaspoons canned salted black
  beans
1 teaspoon soy sauce
1 clove garlic, crushed
½ teaspoon finely grated fresh
  ginger
1 tablespoon dry sherry
125 ml (4 fl oz) cold Chicken Stock
  (see Basics p. 90)
1 teaspoon cornflour
1 tablespoon oil

Cut the chicken meat into 2-cm (¾-in) dice. Cut the celery into thin diagonal slices. Rinse the black beans and mash with a fork. Add the soy sauce, garlic, ginger, sherry and half the Chicken Stock; mix well. Stir the cornflour into the remaining Chicken Stock.

Heat the oil in a wok, add the chicken and stir-fry, tossing for 2 minutes. Pour in the black bean mixture and stir until boiling. Add the cornflour mixture, stirring constantly, until it boils and thickens—about 1 minute. Add the celery slices and toss in the sauce for 1 minute more. Serve immediately with steamed rice.

thai
grilled pepper chicken

Robustly flavoured with garlic, pepper and coriander, it is not for the faint hearted. Works well on a barbecue.

serves 6 to 8

Preparation: 15 mins
Marinating: 60 mins
    minimum, longer is
    preferable
Cooking: 10 mins

**2 kg (4 lb) chicken breast or thigh
    fillets
3 tablespoons Thai Barbecue
    Marinade (see Basics p. 89)**

Wash and dry the chicken fillets, trimming off any visible fat. Lightly score the surface. Rub Thai Barbecue Marinade over the chicken and allow to stand for a couple of hours before cooking, or cover well and refrigerate overnight. Cook the chicken on a barbecue over glowing coals or under a preheated grill for about 5 minutes each side, or until well browned. Garnish, if you wish, with tomato wedges and cucumber slices. Serve with boiled rice or a crisp green salad.

braised spinach with pork

serves 4

Preparation: 15 mins
Cooking: 12 mins

2 bunches fresh spinach, well
    washed or 2 packets frozen
    spinach
500 g (1 lb) pork fillet
2 tablespoons oil
2 cloves garlic, finely chopped
2 tablespoons light soy sauce
    ground black pepper to taste
4 spring onions, finely chopped
2 tablespoons crushed sesame
    seeds, toasted

Remove the tough stems from the spinach and break the leaves into large pieces. Cut the pork into very small dice. Heat the oil in a wok or heavy pan and fry the pork and garlic, stirring constantly, until pork changes colour. Add the spinach and toss well. Season with soy sauce and pepper. Cover and simmer until the spinach is tender—this will only take a short time. Add the spring onions and stir well over a medium heat for 2 minutes. Sprinkle with sesame seeds and serve hot.

stir-fried pork with capsicums

serves 4

Preparation: 20 mins
Freezing: 60 mins
(optional)
Cooking: 7 mins

375 g (12 oz) pork fillet
1 teaspoon finely grated fresh
  ginger
1 clove garlic
½ teaspoon salt
½ teaspoon five-spice powder
2 cups yellow, red or green
  capsicums, cut in squares

2 medium onions, cut into
  4 wedges
2 tablespoons light soy sauce
2 teaspoons cornflour
2 teaspoons oriental sesame oil
2 tablespoons peanut oil

Cut the pork into paper-thin slices (this is easier if you partially freeze the meat until just firm). Combine the ginger, garlic crushed with salt, and five-spice powder. Rub over the sliced pork, cover and set aside for 10 minutes. Prepare the vegetables. Cut the onion wedges into halves crossways and separate into layers. Have all ingredients assembled within reach of where you will be cooking. Combine the soy sauce with 2 tablespoons water, cornflour and sesame oil.

Heat the wok, add 1 tablespoon oil and, when the oil is very hot, fry the onion and capsicum for 1 minute. Remove to a plate at once. Add the remaining tablespoon of oil and when very hot add the pork and stir-fry, tossing and stirring constantly, until it is no longer pink—about 3 or 4 minutes depending on the cooktop (electricity will take longer than gas). Stir the soy sauce mixture as cornflour will have settled, and pour into wok. Stir constantly until the sauce boils and thickens, return the vegetables and toss for 10 seconds to combine. Serve immediately with steamed rice.

steamed chicken

serves 4

Preparation: 5 mins
Cooking: 15 mins

**1 kg (2 lb) chicken pieces (thigh
    cutlets, drumsticks, wings)**
1 tablespoon soy sauce
1 tablespoon dry sherry
2 teaspoons cornflour
**2 teaspoons finely grated fresh
    ginger**
1 teaspoon sugar
1 teaspoon oriental sesame oil

Using a sharp, heavy cleaver, chop the chicken pieces straight through the bones into bite-sized pieces. Combine all the remaining ingredients and mix with chicken pieces. Place on a heatproof dish and put the dish in a steamer over a pan of boiling water. (A bamboo steamer is ideal but a trivet in a large pan will do.) Cover with the lid and steam over a high heat for 15 minutes. Place some chopped vegetables around the chicken before steaming, if preferred. Serve with steamed rice.

chicken with almonds and broccoli

serves 6

Preparation: 10 mins
Cooking: 10 mins

750 g (1½ lb) chicken breast fillets
3 teaspoons cornflour
1 teaspoon five-spice powder
salt to taste
peanut oil
155 g (5 oz) blanched almonds
1 tablespoon dry sherry

1 tablespoon light soy sauce
1 teaspoon sugar
2 teaspoons cornflour
125 g (4 oz) broccoli florets
1 teaspoon finely grated fresh
ginger
½ teaspoon crushed garlic

Cut chicken into 1-cm (½-in) squares. Mix cornflour, five-spice powder and salt together.

Sprinkle over chicken and mix well. In a wok, deep-fry almonds over a medium heat until golden, stirring constantly. Drain on paper towels. Pour off the oil and wipe out the wok with a paper towel.

Mix the sherry, soy sauce, sugar, cornflour and 3 tablespoons cold water, until sugar

dissolves. Heat 2 tablespoons peanut oil in the wok and stir-fry broccoli over a high heat for 2 minutes. Transfer to plate. Add another 2 tablespoons oil and fry ginger and garlic for a few seconds. Toss in the chicken and fry, stirring until chicken changes colour—1 to 2 minutes. Stir reserved sauce mixture and add to the wok, stirring until liquid boils and thickens. Mix in the almonds and broccoli and serve immediately with rice.

honey
soy chicken wings

The flavours in this dish are made for children—even toddlers love to pick up the wings and nibble.

serves 6 to 8

Preparation: 10 mins
Marinating: 60 mins
Cooking: 50 mins

1.5 kg (3 lb) chicken wings
4 tablespoons dark soy sauce
2 tablespoons honey
2 tablespoons dry sherry
2 tablespoons peanut oil
2 teaspoons oriental sesame oil
1 clove garlic, crushed
1 teaspoon finely grated fresh ginger
½ teaspoon five-spice powder
fresh coriander leaves

Wash and dry the wings, cut off and discard the wing tips. Combine all the other ingredients and marinate the wings for 1 hour. Place in a single layer in a roasting dish. Roast in preheated oven at 180°C (350°F) for 35 minutes. Turn the wings over using tongs, brush with any remaining marinade and roast for further 20 minutes or until wings are brown and glazed. Serve warm, garnished with coriander leaves and accompanied by rice.

citrus
chicken and pine nuts

serves 4 to 6

Preparation: 10 mins
Chilling: 30 mins
Cooking: 10 mins

750 g (1½ lb) chicken thigh fillets
1 teaspoon salt
1 tablespoon dry sherry
1 egg white
1 tablespoon cornflour
3 tablespoons peanut oil
30 g (1 oz) pine nuts
1 teaspoon oriental sesame oil
6 slices orange or lemon

Sauce

125 ml (4 fl oz) orange juice, strained
2 tablespoons lemon juice
1 tablespoon sugar
2 teaspoons light soy sauce
1 tablespoon cornflour

Cut the chicken into bite-sized pieces. Season with salt and sherry, pour unbeaten egg white over and mix well. Leave for 10 minutes. Sprinkle with cornflour, add 1 tablespoon peanut oil and mix again. Cover and chill for at least 30 minutes.

Bring plenty of lightly salted water to the boil in the wok and drop in a third of the chicken pieces, stirring until they turn white. Remove with slotted spoon and drain in colander. Repeat with remaining chicken.

Combine Sauce ingredients with 125 ml (4 fl oz) water. Heat remaining oil in the wok and fry the pine nuts over a medium heat until golden. Transfer to paper towel and wipe out wok. Stir the reserved Sauce mixture and pour into the wok. Cook, stirring constantly, until it boils and thickens. Add the sesame oil. Return the chicken and pine nuts to the wok, heat through and serve immediately garnished with orange or lemon slices.

chicken
in peanut sauce

serves 6

Preparation: 10 mins
Marinating: 20 mins
Cooking: 20 mins

1 kg (2 lb) chicken half-breasts on
  the bone
2 small cloves garlic, crushed
1 teaspoon finely grated fresh
  ginger
1 tablespoon Thai Red Curry Paste
  (see Basics p. 89)
2 tablespoons peanut oil
6 spring onions, cut into small
  pieces

3 tablespoons crunchy peanut
  butter
2 teaspoons palm sugar or brown
  sugar
1 tablespoon fish sauce
185 ml (6 fl oz) canned coconut milk
2 cups snake beans or green
  beans, cut into short lengths

Chop each half-breast in two. Mix the garlic, ginger and curry paste and rub into the chicken pieces. Allow to marinate for 20 minutes.

Heat the oil in a wok. Add the spring onions stirring for a few seconds, then remove. Fry the chicken pieces, turning until evenly browned. Mix the peanut butter, sugar, fish sauce and canned coconut milk with 125 ml (4 fl oz) water. (If your brand of coconut milk is very thin, don't add water but use more coconut milk.) Stir until the sugar dissolves, pour into the wok and bring to the boil. Cover and cook gently until the chicken is tender, stirring occasionally and adding a little water if sauce reduces too much. Blanch the green beans, drain and add with the spring onions to chicken. Gently mix together. Serve with steamed rice and a salad.

honey

and sesame chicken

serves 6

Preparation: 5 mins
Marinating: 30 mins
Cooking: 10 mins

750 g (1½ lb) chicken fillets
 few celery leaves
1 large onion, halved
1 teaspoon honey
1 tablespoon oyster sauce
2 tablespoons light soy sauce
 salt to taste
¼ teaspoon five-spice powder
3 spring onions, finely chopped
1 tablespoon finely grated fresh
 ginger
1 tablespoon sesame seeds,
 toasted

Place the chicken fillets in a saucepan with water to cover. Add the celery leaves and onion
and slowly bring just to simmering point. Cover and poach over a very gentle heat for 6 to 8 minutes.
Turn off the heat and allow the chicken to cool in the liquid. (Strain the liquid, chill, then skim off fat.
Reserve this stock for a future use.) Slice the meat thinly. Arrange on a platter.

Mix the honey, oyster sauce, soy sauce, salt and five-spice powder in a small bowl until
well blended. Spoon over the chicken. Cover and leave for 30 minutes. Before serving, mix the spring
onions and ginger and sprinkle over chicken. Top with sesame seeds.

red-cooked chicken drumsticks

'Red cooking' refers to cooking in dark soy sauce. Chicken drumsticks cooked in this manner make ideal picnic food. Freeze or refrigerate leftover cooking liquid. If refrigerating, keep this 'Master Sauce' alive by cooking meat or poultry in it at least once a week.

serves 4 to 6

Preparation: 5 mins
Cooking: 30 mins

2 kg (4 lb) chicken drumsticks
375 ml (12 fl oz) dark soy sauce
125 ml (4 fl oz) dry sherry
5-cm (2-in) piece fresh ginger, sliced
1 clove garlic, bruised
10 small sections star anise
1 tablespoon sugar
2 teaspoons oriental sesame oil

Wash the drumsticks and dry on paper towels. Place in saucepan or flameproof casserole just large enough so that chicken is covered with the cooking sauce. Add 375 ml (12 fl oz) water and remaining ingredients except the sesame oil. Bring slowly to the boil, cover pan and simmer gently for 30 minutes or until tender.

With tongs, turn drumsticks over during cooking. If any pieces are not submerged, rearrange during cooking time. Turn off the heat and leave to cool in the covered saucepan. Lift the chicken pieces from the sauce and transfer to a serving platter. Brush with the sesame oil and serve at room temperature with a small amount of cooking liquid for dipping.

seafood

thai

fish with coconut milk

serves 4

Preparation: 10 mins
Soaking: 10 mins
Cooking: 20 mins

500 g (1 lb) sea perch, ling or salmon
    fillets
  2 large dried chillies
  2 large cloves garlic
  2 kaffir lime leaves
  1 slice galangal
  2 stalks lemon grass, sliced finely
500 ml (1 pint) canned coconut milk
  2 tablespoons fish sauce

  oil for frying
5 small dried chillies
2 tablespoons chopped roasted
  peanuts
fresh basil sprigs

Remove any bones from the fish and cut the fillets into serving pieces. Discard the stalks and seeds from the large chillies; soak in hot water for 10 minutes. Drain and put into a blender with garlic, lime leaves, galangal and lemon grass, adding a little coconut milk, and blend to a paste.

Heat 250 ml (8 fl oz) coconut milk in a wok over a gentle heat until the oil begins to float on top—about 10 minutes. Add the blended mixture and fry, stirring constantly, until it smells cooked and fragrant.

Add the fish pieces, turning to coat in mixture, then add the remaining coconut milk and fish sauce with 250 ml (8 fl oz) water. Stir to mix and simmer just until the fish is cooked. Heat the oil in a small frying pan and fry the small chillies for a few seconds. Set aside. Add the peanuts to the fish just before the end of cooking time and served garnished with fried chillies and basil.

deep-fried fish with vegetables

Accompany this dish with rice or noodles.

serves 4

Preparation: 20 mins
Cooking: 10 mins

750 g (1½ lb) white fish fillets
1 teaspoon salt
2 teaspoons five-spice powder
3 tablespoons cornflour
1 egg white, slightly beaten
oil for frying
extra teaspoon cornflour
1 clove garlic, crushed

½ teaspoon finely grated fresh ginger
2 cups Chinese white cabbage, sliced
6 spring onions, sliced in 5-cm (2-in) lengths
1 tablespoon light soy sauce
1 tablespoon oyster sauce

Cut the fish fillets into finger-sized pieces, discarding any bones. Mix the salt, five-spice powder and cornflour in a large bag. Pour the egg white over the fish and mix. Drop the fish pieces into the bag and shake well to coat. Dust off excess cornflour.

Heat the oil in a wok and fry the fish on a high heat—about one quarter at a time—just until cooked through. This should take 1 to 2 minutes. Remove with slotted spoon as it cooks and drain on a paper towel; keep warm. Mix teaspoon of cornflour with 1 tablespoon of cold water; set aside.

Pour off all but 1 tablespoon of oil from the wok. Add the garlic, ginger and cabbage; stir-fry for 1 minute. Add the spring onions and stir-fry for 1 minute more. Push to the side of the wok. Add the soy and oyster sauces and 125 ml (4 fl oz) water; bring the liquid to the boil and add the cornflour mixture. Stir until the sauce boils and thickens. Pour into a dish, arrange fish pieces on top and serve immediately.

thai
prawn curry

serves 4

Preparation: 10 mins
Cooking: 20 mins

750 g (1½ lb) raw prawns
250 ml (8 fl oz) canned coconut milk
   (see Note)
2 tablespoons Thai Red Curry
   Paste (see Basics p. 89)
4 teaspoons fish sauce
2 fresh red chillies, seeded
2 teaspoons palm sugar
   or brown sugar
4 kaffir lime leaves
   few small basil leaves

Shell and devein the prawns, reserving the heads. Discard the hard top shell from the prawn heads and wash the heads thoroughly. Put the coconut milk in a wok and heat to boiling. Add the curry paste and fry, stirring constantly, until thick and oily. Stir in 250 ml (8 fl oz) water, fish sauce, chilli, palm sugar and lime leaves. Bring slowly to a simmer, stirring.

Add the prawn heads and cook, uncovered, stirring frequently, on a low heat until the heads are cooked and flavours mellow—about 15 minutes. (The prawn heads are edible and have a wonderful flavour.) Add the shelled prawns and cook for 5 minutes more or until prawns change colour and flesh becomes opaque. Sprinkle with basil leaves and serve hot with white rice.

Note Canned coconut milks vary a lot in thickness, and this recipe is based on a rich, thick coconut milk. If you open the can and find it is thin and watery, simply use two cups of coconut milk and omit or reduce the amount of water.

stir-fried prawns and chinese greens

serves 6

Preparation: 20 mins
Cooking: 7 mins

750 g large raw prawns
2 choy sum (flowering cabbage)
   or gai choy (mustard cabbage)
185 ml (6 fl oz) Chicken Stock (see
   Basics p. 90)
2 tablespoons light soy sauce
1 teaspoon five-spice powder

3 tablespoons dry sherry
2 teaspoons cornflour
1 tablespoon peanut oil
3 cloves garlic, crushed
2 teaspoons finely grated
   fresh ginger

Shell and devein the prawns. Cut the choy sum or gai choy into bite-sized pieces, using the thick stems and only the tender part of the leaves. In a small bowl combine the stock, soy sauce, five-spice powder and sherry. Mix cornflour with 2 tablespoons cold water.

Heat the oil in a wok. Add the garlic, ginger and cabbage and fry for 2 minutes over a high heat, stirring constantly. Add the prawns and fry until pink. Lower the heat to medium, add the mixed seasonings. Cover and simmer for 2 minutes. Add the cornflour mixture and stir until the sauce boils and thickens, about 1 minute. Serve at once.

thai
fish in red sauce

It sounds as if it may be hot, but this dish is red from tomatoes not chillies.

serves 4

Preparation: 10 mins
Cooking: 25 mins

4 tablespoons oil
2 onions, finely chopped
4 ripe tomatoes, peeled and
    chopped
2 tablespoons vinegar
    salt and pepper to taste
2 fresh red chillies, seeded and
    chopped
750 g (1½ lb) fish fillets
4 tablespoons chopped fresh
    coriander leaves

Heat the oil in a pan and fry the onion over a moderate heat until soft and golden brown. Add the tomatoes, vinegar, salt, pepper and chilli. Cover the pan and simmer for 20 minutes, or until tomatoes form a pulp and sauce is thick. Add the fish fillets, spooning some of the sauce over. Cover and cook until the fish is done—the flesh will be opaque. The fish will be ready in only a short cooking time, so be careful not to overcook. Serve hot with steamed rice and garnished with coriander leaves.

fish
in spiced yoghurt

This North Indian dish is aromatic without being too fiery. Serve it hot with rice and accompanied by pickles for those who crave extra heat.

serves 4 to 6

Preparation: 10 mins
Cooking: 15 mins

750 g (1½ lb) fish fillets
    salt and freshly ground black
      pepper to taste
1 teaspoon ground turmeric
    oil for frying
2 medium onions, roughly
    chopped
2 cloves garlic
3 teaspoons chopped fresh ginger

2 tablespoons ground almonds
3 teaspoons ground coriander
2 teaspoons ground cummin
1 teaspoon Garam Masala
    (see Basics p. 88)
125 ml (4 fl oz) plain yoghurt
1 tablespoon chopped fresh mint
    leaves

Wash the fillets, dry and cut into large chunks, removing any bones. Combine the salt, pepper and turmeric and rub over the fish. Heat the oil for shallow frying. Seal the fish quickly on both sides over a high heat. Transfer to a plate.

Purée the onions, garlic, ginger, almonds and spices in a blender, adding a little water if necessary to keep the mixture moving. Drain all but 2 tablespoons oil from the pan and fry the purée, stirring constantly, until the colour changes and it smells fragrant.

Swirl 60 ml (2 fl oz) water in a blender to catch any traces of spices, stir into the yoghurt and add. Simmer for a few minutes. Return fish pieces, turning gently to coat with sauce. Add salt to taste. Simmer, covered, for 10 minutes. Serve hot sprinkled with chopped mint and accompanied by rice.

salads & vegetables

beef salad

serves 4

Preparation: 10 mins
Marinating: 15 mins
Cooking: 7 mins

500 g (1 lb) tender, lean grilling
  steak
2 teaspoons Thai Green Curry
  Paste (see Basics p. 90)
1 clove garlic, crushed
1 tablespoon chopped mint or
  coriander leaves
  freshly ground black pepper to
  taste
1 tablespoon palm sugar or brown
  sugar

2 teaspoons Maggi Seasoning
  (see Note)
1 tablespoon lime juice
2 teaspoons fish sauce
½ teaspoon finely grated lime zest
8 small purple shallots, finely
  sliced or 4 spring onions, sliced
2 small seedless cucumbers,
  scored and sliced
  few sprigs fresh mint

Rub the steak with the curry paste, leave for 15 minutes. If you like a barbecued flavour,

cook beef over glowing coals, alternatively grill until medium rare. Slice thinly when cool and firm.

Combine the garlic, mint or coriander, pepper, palm sugar, Maggi Seasoning, lime juice,

fish sauce and lime zest. Place all ingredients in a bowl and toss lightly to distribute dressing.

Note Maggi Seasoning is very similar in flavour to a Thai ingredient, Golden Mountain Sauce, and

a lot more readily obtainable in Western supermarkets.

asparagus salad

serves 4

Preparation: 10 mins
Cooking: 5 mins

2 bunches fresh green asparagus
  or 500 g (1 lb) green beans
375 ml (12 fl oz) strained, cold
  Chicken Stock
  (see Basics p. 90)
2 tablespoons sesame seeds
1 teaspoon sugar
1½ tablespoons light soy sauce
3 teaspoons white wine vinegar
1½ tablespoons water

If using beans, top, tail and cut diagonally into even lengths. Snap the tough ends off the asparagus and discard. Cut into long diagonal slices. Blanch vegetables in boiling water 1 to 2 minutes, until tender but still crisp. Drain, place in a bowl and cover immediately with stock. Leave to cool in the stock.

Toast sesame seeds in a dry pan over a moderate heat, stirring until all are evenly golden brown. Cool on a plate. Crush in blender or mortar and pestle. Mix in remaining ingredients. Drain vegetables well and, just before serving, pour dressing over.

chicken
and cucumber salad

serves 4

Preparation: 10 mins
Cooking: 10 mins

500 g (1 lb) chicken breast fillets
3 teaspoons fish sauce
3 tablespoons lime juice
2 teaspoons sugar
3 small green seedless
  cucumbers, finely sliced
3 red chillies, seeded and finely
  sliced
lettuce leaves
fresh mint

Poach the chicken breasts. Slice when cool. Combine the fish sauce, lime juice and

sugar, stirring to dissolve sugar. Mix gently with the chicken, cucumber and chillies. Serve on lettuce

leaves, garnished with mint.

mixed fruit salad

serves 6

Preparation: 15 mins

mixed fresh fruit (e.g. slices of
  mango, pineapple, grapefruit
  and orange segments, seedless
  grapes)
½ cup water chestnuts, sliced
2 chicken breasts or fillets,
  poached and sliced
6 cooked, shelled prawns

Dressing

2 tablespoons sugar
2 tablespoons fish sauce
3 tablespoons lime juice
1 clove garlic, crushed

Garnish

2 tablespoons crisp-fried shallots
4 tablespoons roasted, salted
  peanuts, crushed
washed lettuce leaves

Line a serving plate with lettuce and cover with the prepared fruits. Combine ingredients for dressing with 3 tablespoons cold water and stir until sugar dissolves. Sprinkle 2 tablespoons over chicken and prawns and toss.

Place the bowl with the remaining dressing on the plate so that it may be spooned over individual servings. Serve sprinkled with shallots and peanuts.

chicken
and cabbage salad

serves 4 to 6

Preparation: 15 mins
Cooking: 10 mins
Marinating: 10 mins

half a Chinese white cabbage
500 g (1 lb) chicken thigh fillets
salt and pepper to taste
1 medium onion, sliced thinly
2 tablespoons sugar
2 tablespoons fish sauce
3 tablespoons lime juice
1 tablespoon white wine vinegar
½ cup chopped mint
¼ cup chopped coriander

Cut the cabbage in halves lengthwise, wash in cold water and shake out all the water. Place cut surface down on a wooden board and, with a sharp knife, cut across into very thin slices. Cover and chill.

Gently simmer the chicken fillets until tender with just enough water to cover, add salt and pepper to taste. Do not overcook. Allow to cool in liquid.

Sprinkle the onion with ½ teaspoon salt and leave for 10 minutes, then rinse under cold water, squeezing out the juices. Add half the sugar and mix. Combine the remaining sugar, fish sauce, lime juice and vinegar. Slice cooled chicken finely. Just before serving combine all the ingredients including mint and coriander and toss well.

braised
bean curd and vegetables

serves 6

Preparation: 5 mins
Cooking: 10 mins

1 tablespoon peanut oil
1 large clove garlic, crushed
500 g (1 lb) mixed vegetables of
   choice, cut into bite-sized
   pieces—baby corn, snow peas,
   button mushrooms, gai larn
125 ml (4 fl oz) Chicken Stock
   (see Basics p. 90) or vegetable
   stock

2 tablespoons oyster sauce
1 tablespoon soy sauce
1½ tablespoons dry sherry
2 teaspoons cornflour
500 g (1 lb) fresh bean curd, sliced

Heat the oil in a wok, swirling to coat the surface. Add the garlic and fry for 10 seconds.

Add the vegetables and stir-fry for 2 minutes. Add the stock, cover and simmer for 1 minute longer.

Mix the oyster sauce, soy sauce and sherry. Add to the wok, stir and simmer. Mix the cornflour with

1 tablespoon cold water. Add to the wok, stirring until it boils and thickens. Add the bean curd, heat

through and serve immediately.

broccoli chinese style

After trying this recipe, you'll never throw away another broccoli stem.

serves 6

Preparation: 10 mins
Cooking: 5 mins

1 large bunch broccoli
  salt
1 tablespoon peanut oil
1 teaspoon grated fresh ginger
1 tablespoon oyster sauce
1 tablespoon light soy sauce
1 teaspoon sugar
½ teaspoon oriental sesame oil
2 teaspoons cornflour

Cut the flowerheads from the broccoli stems, divide into florets and set aside. Peel the stems and slice into bite-sized pieces, cutting thick stems in half lengthwise. Boil a small amount of lightly salted water in a saucepan and drop in the stems. When water returns to the boil, cover and cook for 1 minute, then add florets. Cook 1 minute or until bright green and just tender. Lift out with a slotted spoon. Reserve 125 ml (4 fl oz) cooking water.

In a wok, heat the peanut oil and stir-fry the ginger for 30 seconds. Add the oyster sauce, soy sauce, sugar, sesame oil and reserved cooking liquid and bring to the boil. Blend the cornflour with 1 tablespoon of cold water, add and stir until it boils and thickens. Toss in the broccoli pieces to coat with sauce and serve hot.

stir-fried lettuce

Especially good in winter when a chilled salad doesn't seem tempting.

serves 6

Preparation: 5 mins
Cooking: 2 mins

1 large, firm iceberg lettuce
1 tablespoon peanut oil
1 teaspoon crushed garlic
1 teaspoon finely grated fresh
   ginger
  salt to taste
1 teaspoon sugar
1 tablespoon light soy sauce

Wash the lettuce and dry well. Cut in half lengthwise, then make 2 or 3 cuts lengthwise and the same across to give chunky, bite-sized pieces.

Heat a wok, add peanut oil, garlic and ginger and stir-fry for 10 seconds, then add the lettuce and stir-fry for a further 30 to 40 seconds. Remove from heat, add salt, sugar and soy sauce. Toss and serve immediately.

braised
mixed vegetables

serves 6 to 8

Preparation: 10 mins
Soaking: 30 mins
  (if using dried shiitake
  mushrooms)
Cooking: 30 mins

12 dried or fresh shiitake (Chinese)
    mushrooms
15 g (½ oz) dried wood fungus
 1 × 550 g (1 lb 3 oz) can winter
    bamboo shoots
 1 × 250 g (8 oz) can water
    chestnuts
 1 × 425 g (15 oz) can young
    corn cobs

3 tablespoons peanut oil
3 tablespoons soy sauce
1 tablespoon sugar
1 star anise
3 slices ginger
3 teaspoons oriental sesame oil

Soak the dried mushrooms in 750 ml (1½ pints) hot water for 30 minutes. Cut off the stems, discard, and squeeze the excess water from the caps, reserving the liquid. Soak the wood fungus in plenty of cold water for 10 minutes, drain, discard gritty bits and cut fungus into bite-sized pieces.

Slice the bamboo shoots and water chestnuts thinly and drain the corn. Heat the wok, add the peanut oil and stir-fry mushrooms, pressing undersides against the wok until golden brown. Add the remaining ingredients except the wood fungus and sesame oil. Pour in 500 ml (16 fl oz) water or mushroom liquid. Cover the wok and simmer for 25 to 30 minutes. Add wood fungus and sesame oil and heat through. Serve with steamed rice.

braised
chinese cabbage

serves 6

Preparation: 8 mins
Cooking: 4 mins

750 g (1½ lb) Chinese white cabbage
(wongah bak) and Chinese
mustard cabbage (gai choy)
1 tablespoon peanut oil
1 teaspoon crushed garlic
1 teaspoon finely grated fresh
ginger
185 ml (6 fl oz) Chicken Stock
(see Basics p. 90)
1½ tablespoons light soy sauce
2 teaspoons cornflour
½ teaspoon oriental sesame oil

Remove any tough leaf tips, leaving a narrow border on the mid rib. Cut into bite-sized pieces. In a wok heat the oil and stir-fry the garlic and ginger for a few seconds, add the cabbage and stir-fry for 1 minute. Add the stock and soy sauce. Cook, covered, for 2 minutes, or until the cabbage is tender but still crunchy. Mix the cornflour with 1 tablespoon cold water and stir into sauce. Cook, stirring, until it boils and thickens. Add the sesame oil, toss to mix and serve.

Any meal can be quick to prepare, but in order to save time when cooking the actual meal, you need to do some thinking ahead and stockpiling—pun intended. (My name for two of my freezer shelves is 'The Stock Market'.) Soup is made in a trice, provided you have stock in the freezer or have purchased good quality stock. It is practical to make chicken stock and beef stock in large quantities (sufficient for at least three meals) and freeze them in meal-sized portions. The best stocks are simmered long and slowly, so why bother with small amounts when it takes the same time to make enough for many meals. The beef stock on which the famous Vietnamese Pho is based (listed here as Beef Soup with Salad) is a perfect example of using time and fuel to good advantage. Another tip to save time and effort is to soak, slice and cook more dried shiitake mushrooms than you need for one recipe. It takes the same time, just increase the amount of soaking liquid, soy sauce and ginger and set aside in the refrigerator for stir-fried dishes.

Another recommendation is that curry pastes and marinades be made in sufficient quantity to provide at least three meals. The time invested is the same, and what this book is all about is getting the best return for your time and effort. For instance the Thai Barbecue Marinade and curry pastes can be prepared and stored in tightly stoppered glass jars in the refrigerator. Use a clean, dry spoon each time some is taken out and it will keep for months.

It is not only making the pastes with the help of a powerful electric blender, but searching out the ingredients which puts busy people off, so I have made my own range of ready to use marinades and pastes which are available from gourmet departments and specialty food stores in Australia. These are based on the same recipes offered in my books, free of artificial additives and chemical flavour enhancers. After opening, store in the refrigerator and remember the rule about using a clean, dry spoon each time. These are a boon to busy people, including myself.

the essentials

Very few kitchen utensils are needed to prepare these quick and easy recipes. The most useful item is the wok as it is designed to distribute heat quickly and requires only a small amount of oil. A large frying pan will do a similar job but won't allow you to toss your vegetables quite as high! A wide Chinese chopper is ideal for chopping ingredients and carrying them to the wok but a good, sharp knife is just as suitable.

To help you prepare and cook the recipes in this book as quickly as possible, a list of the most commonly used herbs and spices has been put together. With a collection of basic herbs and spices in your pantry, you will be able to cook many of the recipes in this book in no time. Don't be put off if you are missing a particular herb or spice — each one adds a little more flavour but as long as it is not a major ingredient the meal will probably be just as tasty without. In some cases ingredients can be substituted with alternatives which may be more likely to be in your kitchen, for example lemon zest instead of lemon grass or peanut butter instead of Chinese sesame paste. The meal may not be quite as authentic, but is still immensley enjoyable.

here is the essential list of herbs and spices

ginger	**basil (fresh)**	**cardamom pods**
garlic	**coriander (fresh)**	**five-spice powder**
	lemon grass (fresh)	**ground cummin**
	kaffir lime leaves	**ground turmeric**
	(fresh or dried)	**sesame seeds**
	mint leaves (fresh)	

spices, pastes and marinades

easy garam masala

2 tablespoons ground coriander
1 tablespoon ground cummin
2 teaspoons ground black pepper
1 tablespoon ground cinnamon
3 teaspoons ground cardamom
1 teaspoon ground cloves
2 teaspoons ground nutmeg

Combine coriander, cummin and pepper and roast in dry pan until fragrant, stirring constantly and using low heat because powder will burn very easily. When they smell fragrant, turn onto a plate. Dry roast remaining spices on very low heat for a minute. Mix, cool completely and bottle airtight.

thai barbecue marinade

One of the most useful items to have in the refrigerator. It keeps very well, but if you don't use it as fast as I do, it may be wise to add 1 teaspoon of citric acid dissolved in a tablespoon or so of hot water.

makes about 1 cup

> 1 tablespoon chopped garlic
> 2 teaspoons salt
> 2 tablespoons whole black peppercorns
> 2 cups coarsely chopped fresh coriander, including roots
> 2 tablespoons lemon juice

Crush the garlic with the salt to a smooth paste. Roast the peppercorns in a dry pan for 1 or 2 minutes, then coarsely crush in a mortar and pestle. Finely chop coriander roots, leaves and stems. Mix all ingredients. You can make this paste in a blender, but reduce black peppercorns to 1 tablespoon, as they are hotter when more finely ground. Store in an airtight jar in the refrigerator.

Note Some of the ways I use this paste include marinating chicken fillets with a good thick coating of it for 15 minutes, then cooking them on the barbecue. Or, if I want a quick green chutney and don't have any fresh herbs on hand, stir a spoonful of the paste into a cup of natural yoghurt. If you run out of Thai Green Curry Paste never hesitate to use Thai Barbecue Marinade instead.

thai red curry paste

Curry paste is not worth making in tiny amounts. It keeps well if stored in a clean, dry, tightly stoppered bottle and refrigerated. Or one can divide it into tablespoon-sized portions and freeze.

makes about 1 cup

> 4 to 6 dried red chillies
> 2 small brown onions, chopped
> 1 teaspoon black peppercorns
> 2 teaspoons ground cummin
> 1 tablespoon ground coriander
> 2 tablespoons chopped fresh coriander, including root
> 1 teaspoon salt
> 1 stem lemon grass, finely sliced, or 2 teaspoons chopped lemon rind
> 2 teaspoons chopped galangal root in brine
> 1 tablespoon chopped garlic
> 2 teaspoons dried shrimp paste
> 1 tablespoon oil
> 1 teaspoon turmeric
> 2 teaspoons paprika (see Note)

Remove the stems from the chillies. If you want the curry to be as hot as it is in Thailand, leave the seeds in, otherwise shake them out. Break the chillies into pieces and soak in just enough hot water to cover for 10 minutes. Place in an electric blender container with all other ingredients. Blend until a smooth paste forms, stopping frequently to add a little water to assist the blending.

Note Though paprika is not used in Thailand, I have added it to give this curry the requisite red colour without using as many chillies as would be used on its home ground.

thai green curry paste

Without the tiny, fiercely hot green chillies used in Thailand this isn't truly authentic, but is still fragrant and full of aroma without the pungent heat.

makes about 1 cup

4 large or 8 small green chillies
1 medium brown onion, chopped
1 tablespoon chopped garlic
1 cup firmly packed fresh coriander including roots
3 tablespoons finely sliced lemon grass or thinly peeled zest of one lemon
2 tablespoons chopped galangal, fresh or bottled
2 teaspoons ground coriander
1 teaspoon ground cummin
1 teaspoon black peppercorns
1 teaspoon ground turmeric
1 teaspoon dried shrimp paste
60 ml (2 fl oz) lemon juice
½ teaspoon citric acid

Remove the stems and seeds, chop chillies roughly and blend with all other ingredients in food processor or blender to a smooth paste. Store in clean, dry glass jar in refrigerator for 4 or 5 weeks and always use a clean, dry spoon to measure amount required. Or divide into portions, wrap and freeze.

stocks

beef stock

2 kg (4 lb) beef brisket on the bone
500 g (1 lb) shin beef
2 onions, sliced
5-cm (2-in) piece fresh ginger, sliced
stick of cinnamon
5 whole star anise
1 teaspoon whole black peppercorns

Put the beef in a large saucepan. Add cold water to cover with onions, ginger, cinnamon, star anise and peppercorns. Bring to the boil, turn heat very low, cover and simmer for 6 hours. Add salt to taste. Strain, chill and remove fat, then freeze in meal-sized portions.

chicken stock

Usually a flavour base for soups, served alone it makes an ideal dieter's chicken broth. Serve sprinkled with a few chopped coriander leaves or finely sliced spring onions. It is also suitable for use in Thai soup recipes.

2 kg (4 lb) chicken bones, including neck and feet
20 black peppercorns
4 small stalks celery with leaves
2 onions
few stalks fresh coriander, including root
4 thick slices fresh ginger
salt to taste

Place the chicken bones in a saucepan with 4 litres (128 fl oz) cold water and remaining ingredients. Bring to the boil, skimming if necessary. Cover and simmer for 45 minutes to 1 hour. Strain and chill. Any fat will congeal on surface and can be easily removed. Freeze in meal-sized portions.

rice and noodles

steamed rice

Whatever kind of rice you cook, it is important to use a heavy-based saucepan.
Or use an electric rice cooker with the same amounts of rice and cold water.

500 g (1 lb) short or medium grain rice
750 ml (1½ pints) cold water

If necessary, wash the rice in cold water. Drain in a sieve or colander for a few minutes. Place rice in a heavy based saucepan with a well-fitting lid. Add 750 ml (24 fl oz) cold water and bring rapidly to the boil. Cover the pan, turn the heat very low and cook for 15 minutes without lifting lid. Remove pan from heat and set aside, covered, for 10 minutes before serving.

Short or medium grain rice, cooked by the absorption method, can accompany Korean, Vietnamese, Chinese and Japanese dishes. It is pearly and clinging and easy to pick up with chopsticks.

Long grain rice, for Indian, Indonesian or Thai meals, will give an aromatic, fluffy result more suited to the cuisine of those countries. Since long grain rice has greater absorbency, increase water slightly to 1 litre (32 fl oz) for 500 g (1 lb) rice.

Natural brown (unpolished) rice has the benefits of extra fibre and B vitamins. Use the same proportions as for long grain rice, but be prepared for it to take almost twice as long to cook, 35 to 40 minutes until all the liquid is absorbed.

egg noodles

Serve these noodles with soups, stir-fried or braised dishes.

Egg noodles are made with wheat flour and usually sold in 500 g (1 lb) packets, each containing about 7 bundles. It is important to soak these noodles in warm water for about 10 minutes before cooking them since the strands separate and cook more evenly. Do this while waiting for your water to come to the boil.
To cook, drain the noodles, drop into boiling water and boil fine noodles for 2 to 3 minutes and wide noodles for 3 to 4 minutes. They should be tender but firm to the bite. Drain immediately in a large colander, then rinse with cold water to get rid of excess starch and to stop the cooking process. Drain thoroughly. You can reheat the noodles in the colander by pouring boiling water over them.

bean thread vermicelli

Use in soups or braised dishes.

Also known as cellophane noodles, transparent noodles, bean starch noodles, bean threads, silver threads, spring rain noodles, harusame or fenszu. Cook in boiling water 10 minutes or until tender. Drain.

index